# Brothers and Sisters

Leon Read

W
FRANKLIN WATTS

# Contents



Look out for Tiger on the pages of this book. Sometimes he is hiding.

Some of us have brothers.
Some of us have sisters.

They are part of the family.

Every family is different.

# Different families

Brothers and sisters
are different too.

I have two brothers.
Who is in your family?

# Just a bump

All babies are born the same way.

Your sister is a girl. Your brother is a boy.

My baby
brother isn't
born yet!

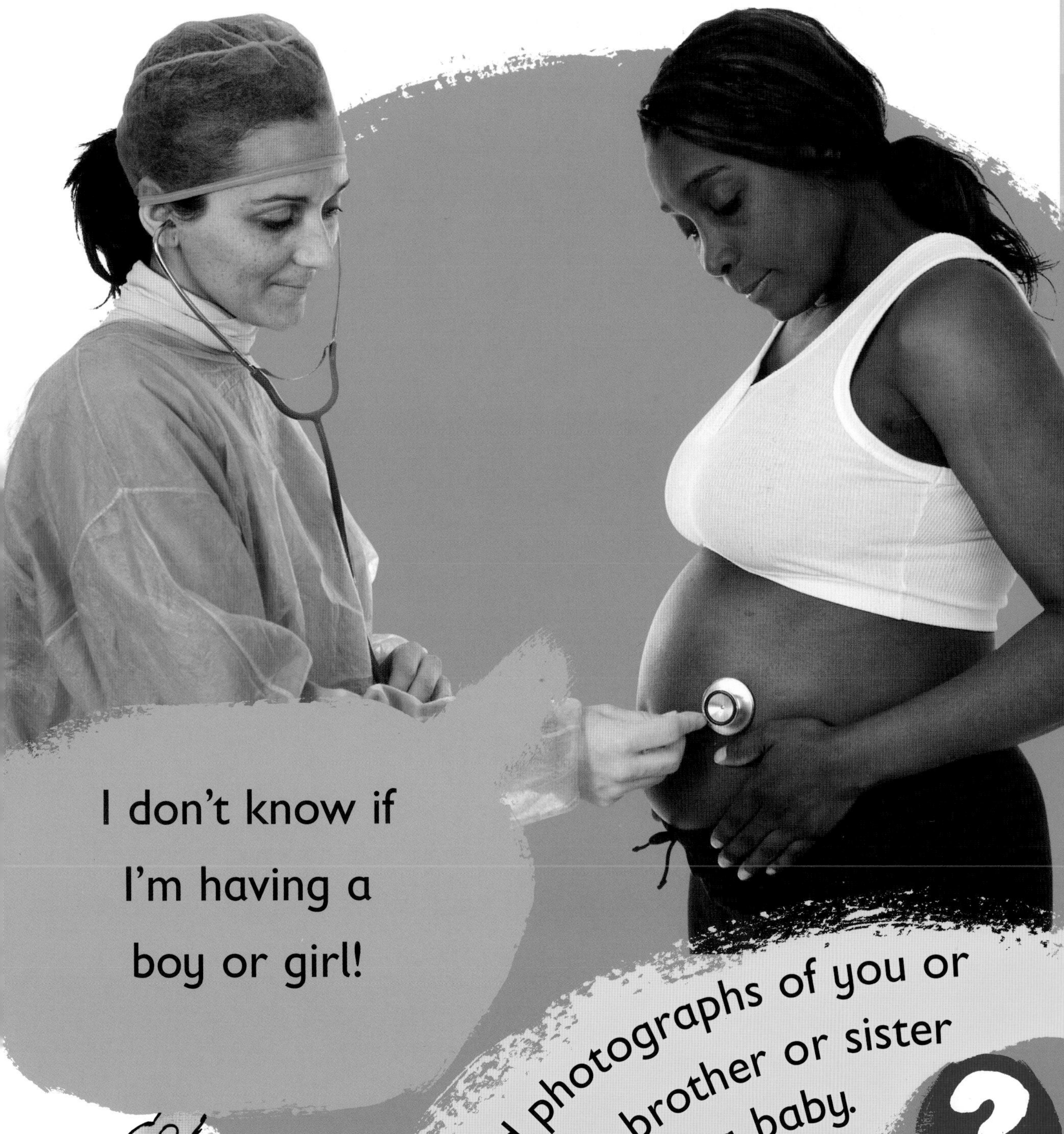

I don't know if
I'm having a
boy or girl!

Find photographs of you or
your brother or sister
as a baby.

# Younger and older

Older brothers and sisters were born before us.

older brother

Younger brothers and sisters were born after us.

younger sister

Do you have a brother or sister? Are they older or younger than you?

# Twins

Some brothers and sisters are born at exactly the same time.

They are called twins.

Some twins look the same as each other and some don't.

Lilly and Rachel are twins.

# Tiger's tale

Tiger doesn't have
a brother or sister.

He still has lots of fun
with his friend Rabbit.

Do your friends have
brothers and sisters?

# Playing pirates

Mica and Freddie are brother and sister.

They love playing pirates together.

The sea monster is coming!
Argh!
Who do you like to play with?
?

# Bedroom fight

Mica shares a bedroom with her sister Shaz.

Mica jumps on Shaz's bed.

Then Shaz
shouts at Mica.

What should Mica do?
What should Shaz do?

# Growing up

Our brothers and sisters grow up with us.

Older brothers and sisters help out.

They are always our brothers and sisters.

Take photographs of your brothers and sisters as they grow up.

# Birthday party

We invite our brothers, sisters and friends to our birthday party.

We celebrate our birthday every year.

We eat birthday cake.

We blow out candles.

What is your favourite thing about birthday parties?

# Making a present

Make a present for your brother or sister, or a friend.

Freddie is making a spoon puppet.

He sticks on some felt hair then adds the eyes and nose.

Now he adds
arms, hands
and a smiley
mouth.

He makes a
felt T-shirt.
Now the
puppet is
finished!

# Word picture bank

Birthday – P. 20

Older – P. 8

Pirate – P. 14

Puppet – P. 22

Twins – P. 10

Younger – P. 9

This edition 2012
First published in 2008 by Franklin Watts
338 Euston Road, London NW1 3BH

Franklin Watts Australia
Level 17/207 Kent Street, Sydney NSW 2000



Series editor: Adrian Cole
Photographer: Andy Crawford (unless otherwise credited)
Design: Sphere Design Associates
Art director: Jonathan Hair
Consultants: Prue Goodwin and Karina Law

A CIP catalogue record for this book is available from the British Library.

ISBN: 978 1 4451 0746 2

Dewey Classification: 306.875

Acknowledgements:
The Publisher would like to thank Norrie Carr model agency. 'Tiger' and 'Rabbit' puppets used with kind permission from Ravensden PLC (www.ravensden.co.uk). Tiger Talk logo drawn by Kevin Hopgood.
Photo credits: cover, 3t, 19 Julián Rovagnati/Shutterstock. 3b, 11 Glenda M. Powers/Shutterstock. 4, 5t, 18b Sonya Etchison/Shutterstock. 5b paulaphoto/Shutterstock. 6 Losevsky Pavel/Shutterstock. 7 Gelpi/Shutterstock. 8, 24tc Pascale Wowak/Shutterstock. 9, 24br Thomas M Perkins/Shutterstock. 10, 24bc Melissa King/Shutterstock. 18t iofoto/Shutterstock. 20, 24tl Jupiter Images/Burke/Triolo Productions. 21l Christina Richards/Shutterstock. 21r Victoria Alexandrova/Shutterstock.



Printed in China

Franklin Watts is a division of Hachette Children's Books, an Hachette UK company.
www.hachette.co.uk